THE WORLD OF
QUINO

THE WORLD OF
QUINO

AN OWL BOOK

HENRY HOLT AND COMPANY / NEW YORK

Library of Congress Catalog Card Number: 86-81207
ISBN 0-8050-0092-5 (pbk.)

First Edition

Printed in the United States of America
1 3 5 7 9 10 8 6 4 2

ISBN 0-8050-0092-5

INTRODUCING

Quino

For over twenty years Quino has been recognized and honored as one of the foremost cartoonists in the world. His strip *Mafalda* and his uncaptioned panels have won him a vast international following.

Joaquin Lavado was born in Mendoza, Argentina, in 1932. His childhood nickname, "Quino," became his pen name when he began his career as a cartoonist at the age of twenty-two. *Mundo Quino,* a collection of wordless cartoons, was published in 1963 and established him as a presence in the Argentine art world.

In 1964 he began his famous comic strip, *Mafalda,* which features the wise but scathing insights of a little girl and her friends. During its nine-year run, the strip became one of the most successful in history, with over 100 million readers throughout South America and Europe. Even today, thirteen years after Quino drew the final strip, *Mafalda* is continually reprinted in newspapers, magazines, and books in South America, Greece, Italy, Portugal, Spain, France, West Germany, Scandinavia, and Canada. *Mafalda* has also appeared as an animated feature.

During the years he was writing and drawing *Mafalda,* Quino continued to draw his eloquent, wordless cartoon panels, and since 1973 that has been his primary focus. They regularly appear in newspapers and magazines in South America and Europe, and have been published in book form in many countries. *The World of Quino* presents a selection of cartoons from the past ten years.

Quino and his wife, Alicia, live in Buenos Aires. He travels widely, and has lived and worked for long periods in Europe, especially in Milan. In 1978 he won the Palma d'Oro award of the International Salon of Humour of Bordighera, Italy, and in 1981 was awarded the Grand Prix de l'Humour Noir in France. In 1982 he was honored as Cartoonist of the Year at the International Salon of Cartoons in Montreal, Canada.

¥1000

nocimiento de la existencia de esos lsos contrapuestos y simultáneos es ave para el entendimiento de la vida ica normal o patológica. La ambi- ncia, es decir la experiencia simultánea afición y la aversión a una misma persona es a su vez el elemento fundamental de la vida afectiva; la admisión de esa ambigüedad de significado, de la coexistencia inseparable de los sentimientos de atracción y de aversión, es requisito indispensable para cualquier entendimiento Muy parecidos son los supuestos que hemos de admitir en relación con la estructura de la vida familiar. Lo que se predica del individuo puede predicarse, por lo menos en sentido figurado, de un grupo de individuos. La situación, en este caso, es paralela a la que plantea la ambivalencia de los sentimientos individuales; se trata, en efecto, de la oposición entre el deseo (y la necesidad) de estar reunido con otras personas y el deseo (y la necesidad) de estar solo y de subsistir por uno mismo. Los dos polos afirmar nuestra propia i individuos y el de enco y seguridad en la dep nadie se le ocurre pen que tendrá para la ma

BOSS M
MAFIOSO
IN BOSS
OSO IN BOS

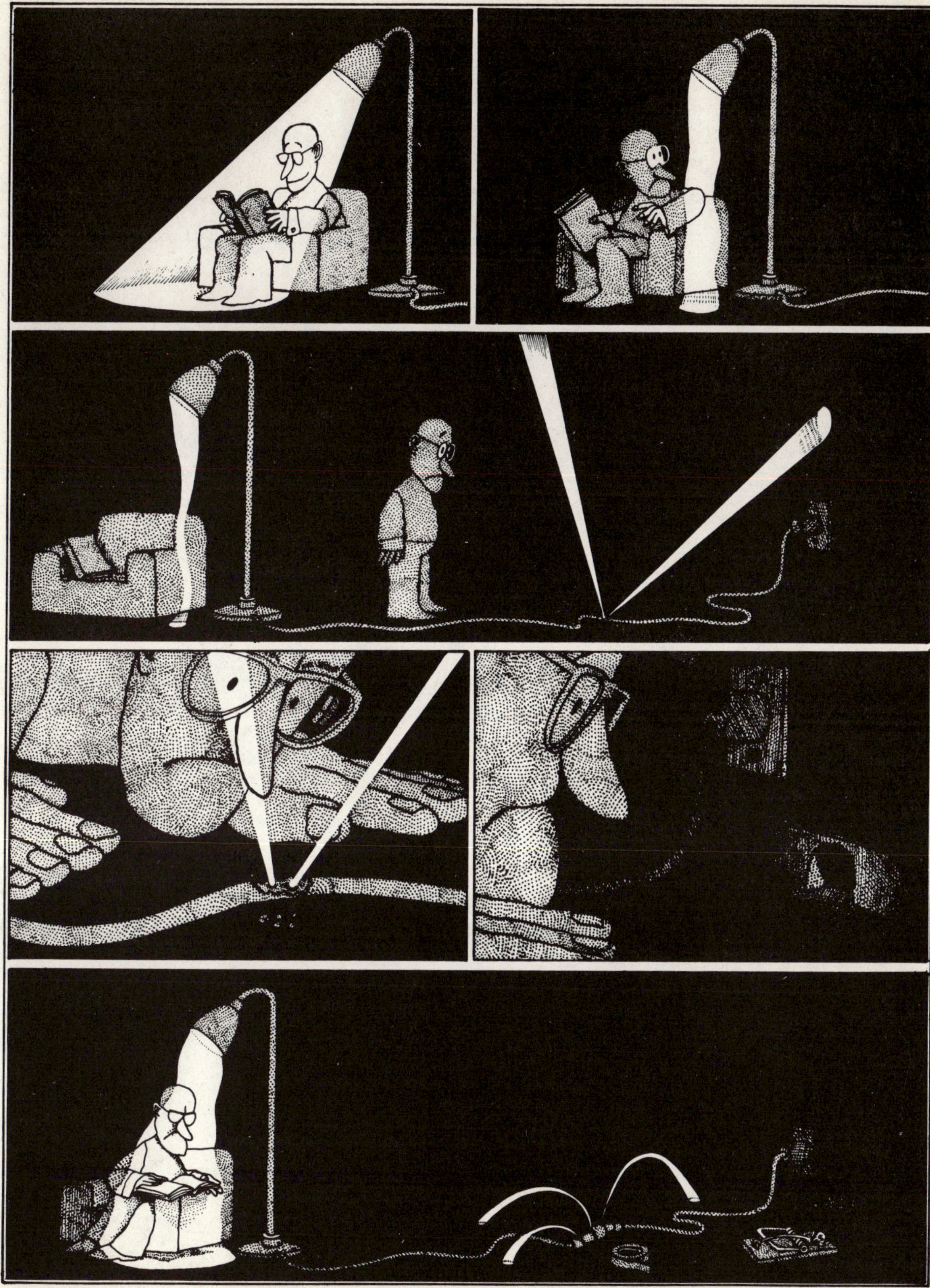

MUPHIS
IX
KERFES
II
TOTIS
IV
MUSEUM
KERFES
II
TOTIS
IV
MUSEUM
TOTIS
IV
MUSEUM
KERFES
II
TOTIS
IV
NAOK
I
MUSEUM

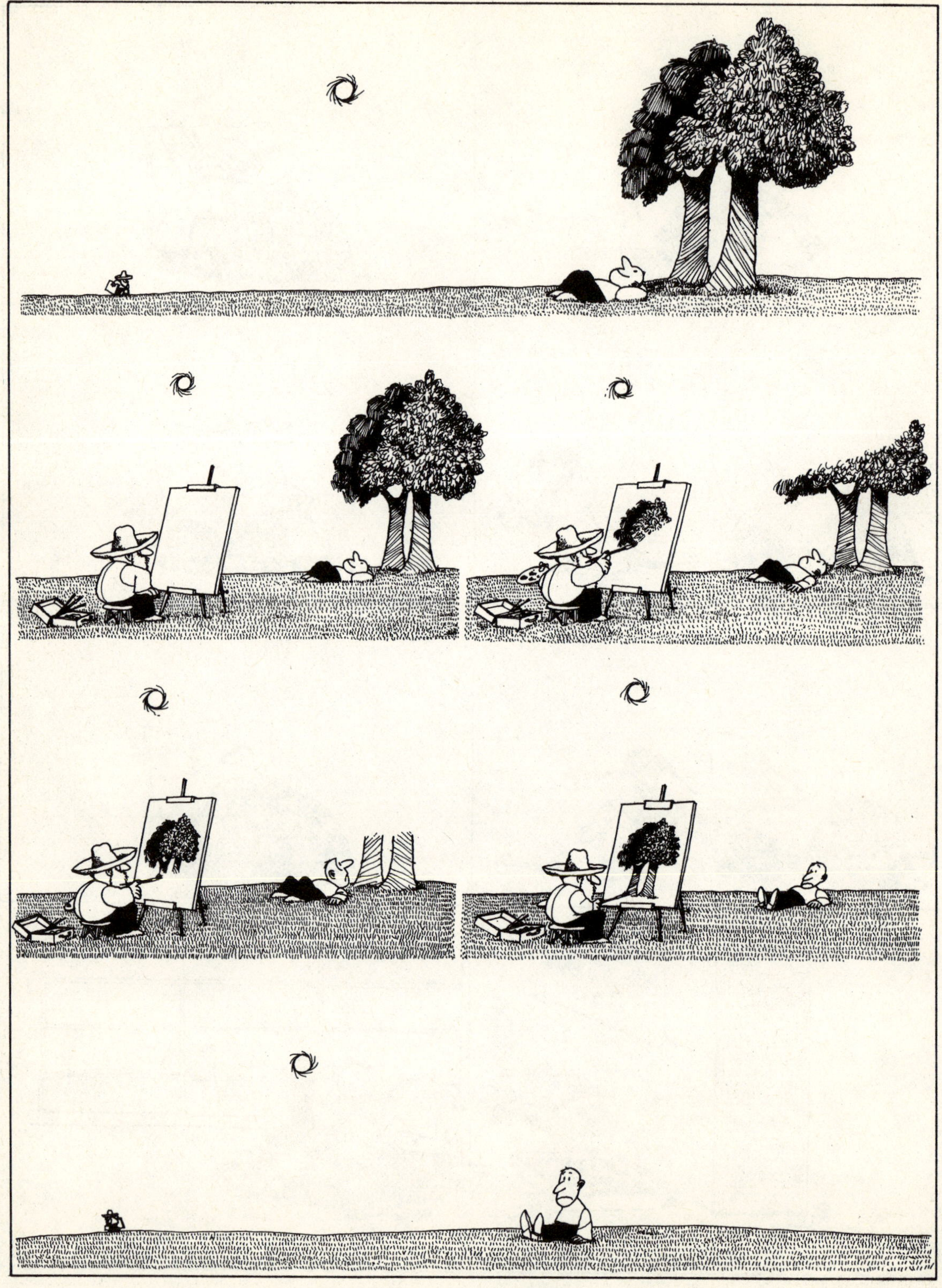

wmw's

QUEJAS

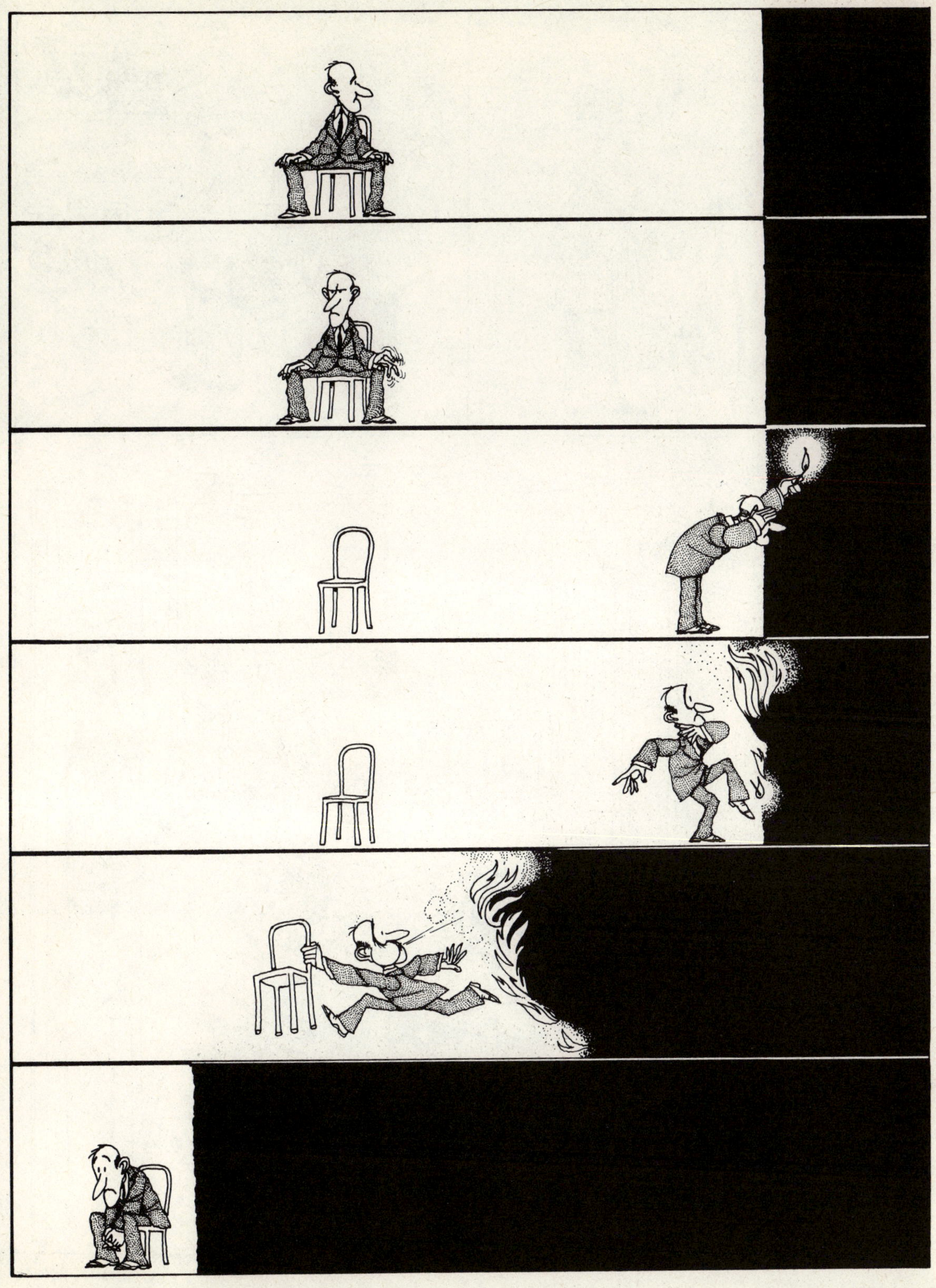

12
TAXI

Poems

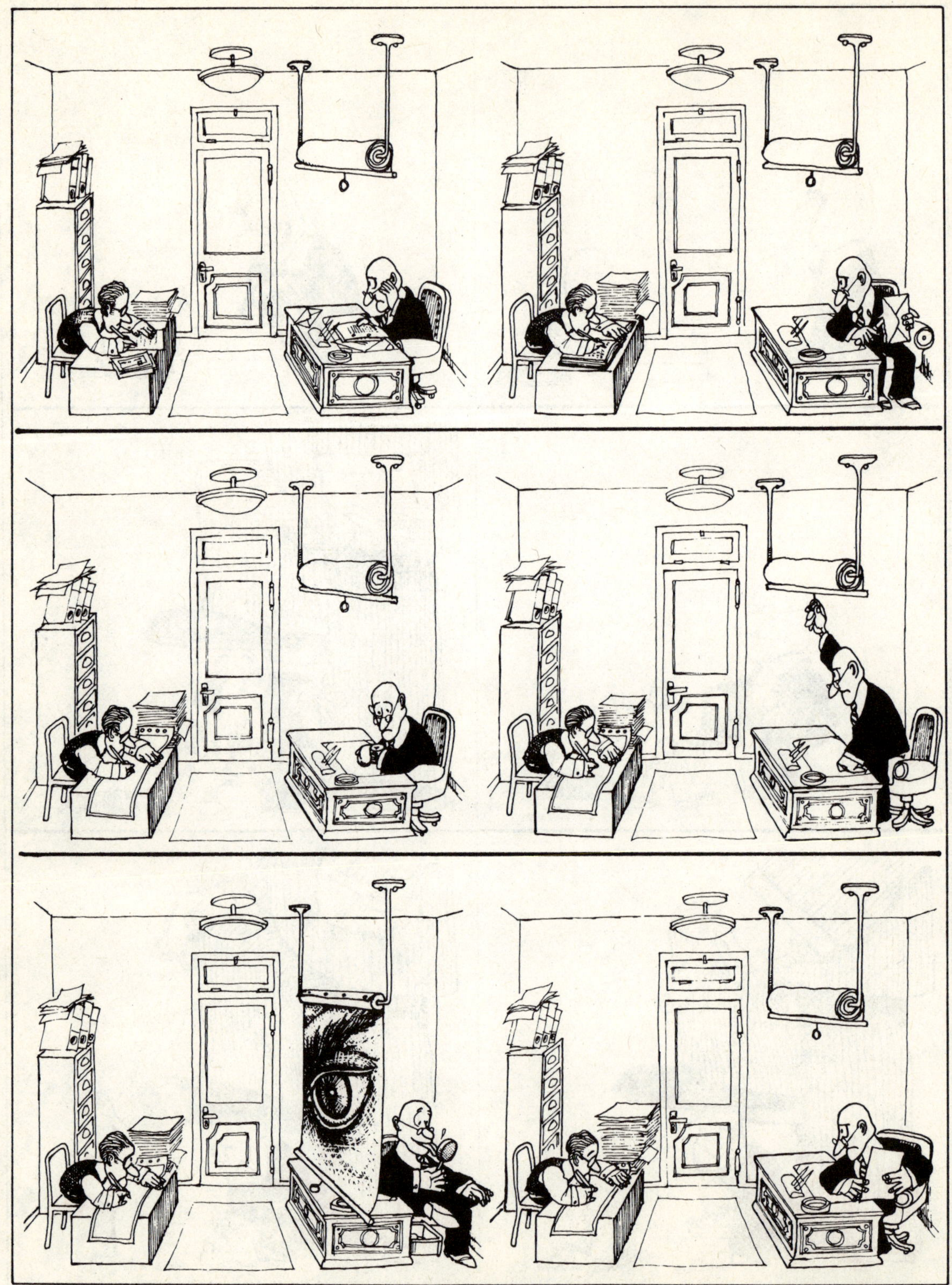

¡PROMM!

HOTEL ZENTRUM

HOTEL

¡OOOÁ́ÁÁ́..……HIÓÓ-HIÓÓ¡

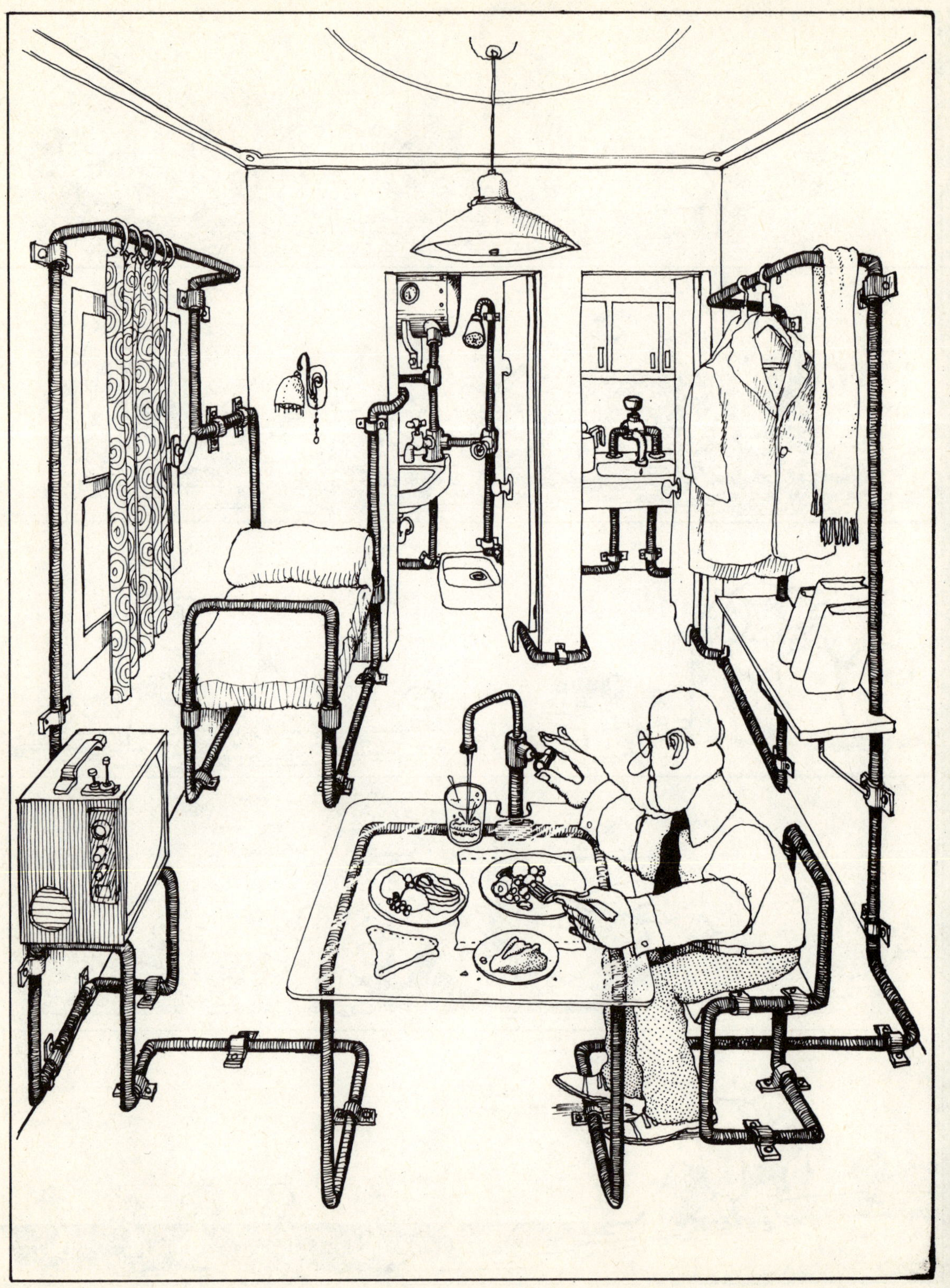

London Paris
RHUM

PFUND
POXING CLUB

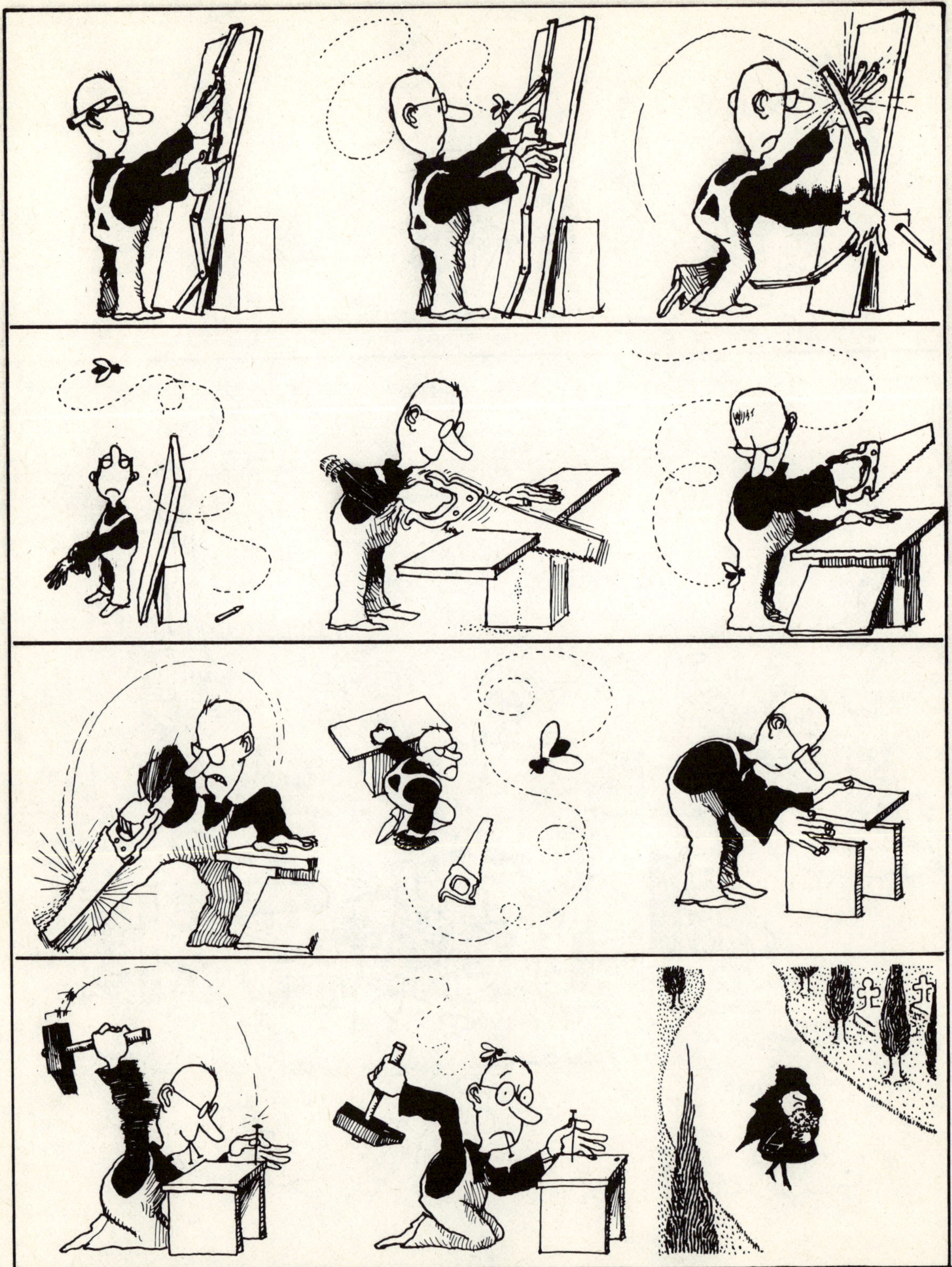

LIMPEY
NUBO

MOIX & FERGUSON · 10° ANIVERSARIO
MOIX &
FERGUSON
60
ANIVERSARIO

COFF!
COFF!
TSSHIIISS!...

2 + 2 = 4
2 + 2 = 4
AMERBANK
FINANCEX
BANCO DE
CREDIT
THE CHICAGO INSTITUTE
CAMBIO CHANGE WECHSEL
DEUTSCHE BANK

M. FUX
ARQUITECTO
CONSTRUCTOR

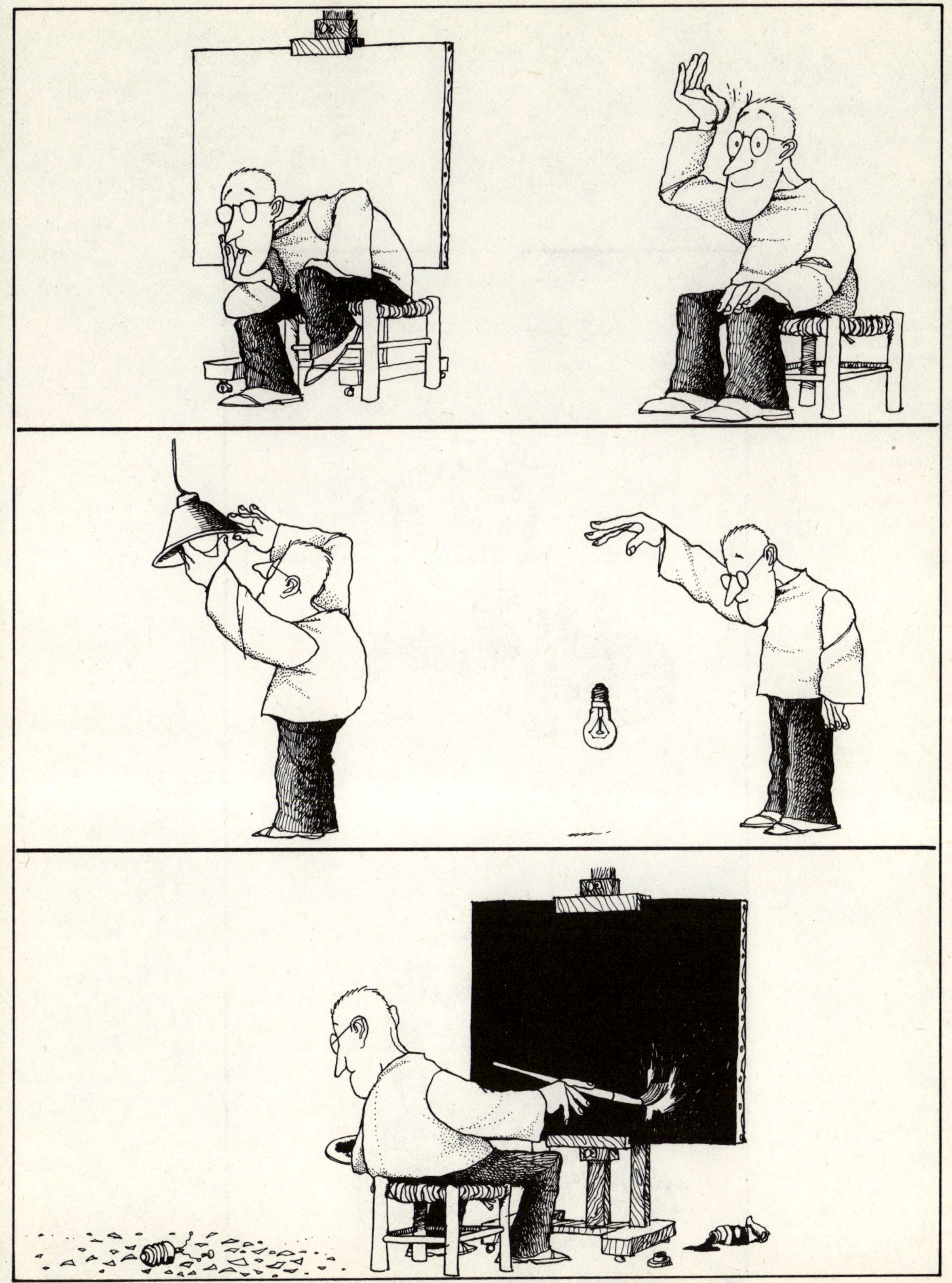

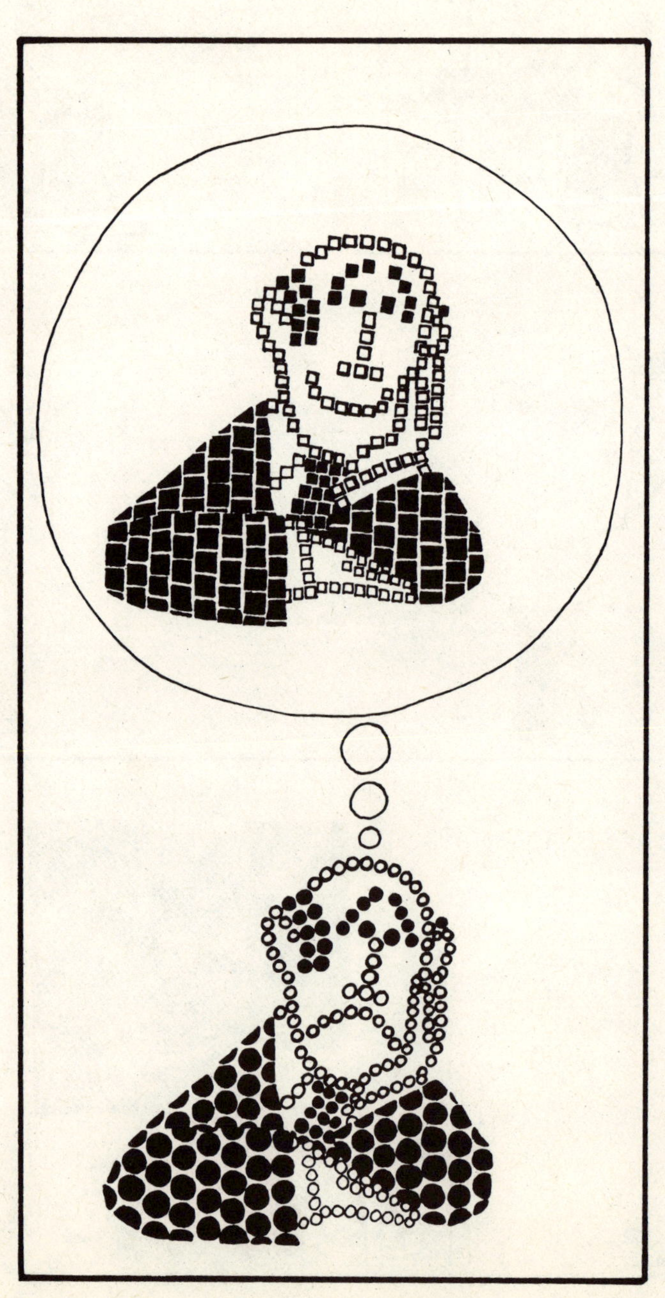

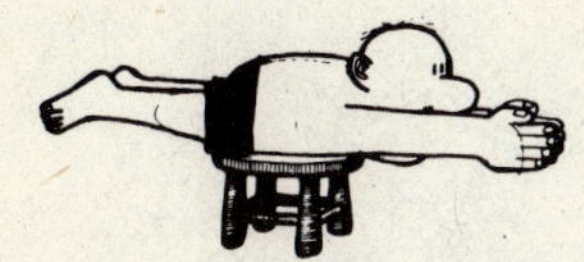
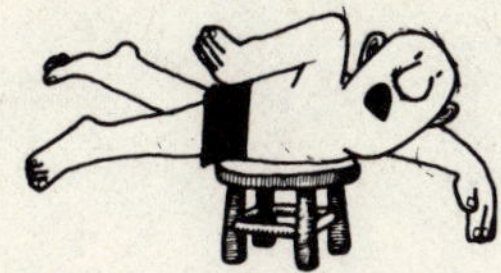
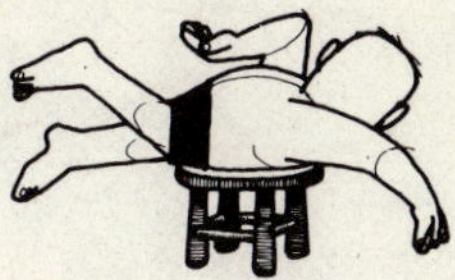
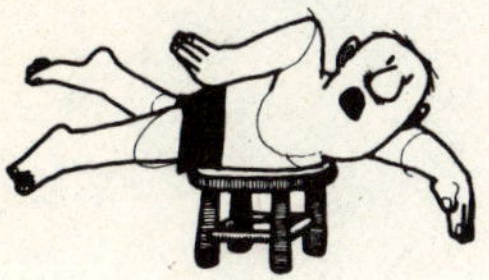
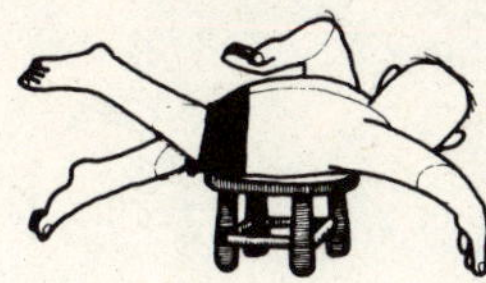

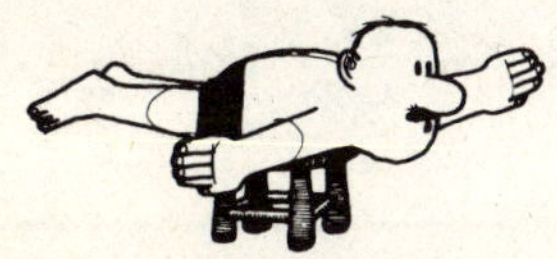

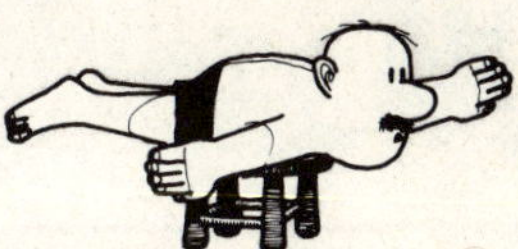

N° 912043

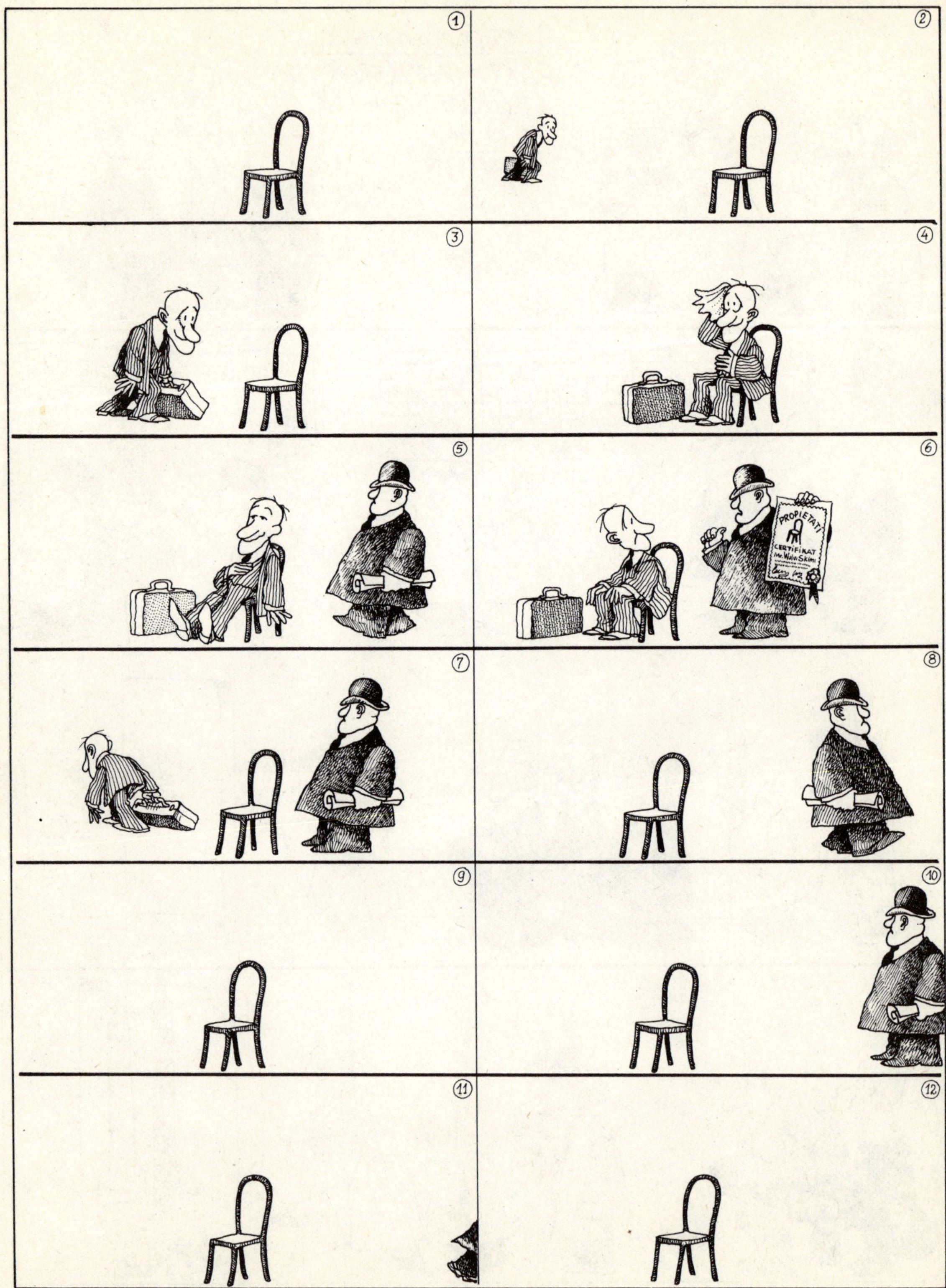

PROPIETATI
CERTIFIKAT
Mr. Waldi Skimi

SX - 120
F 250
KW-1

Mercedes